THE ART DECO CITY
Napier, New Zealand

Robert McGregor

First published 1998 by the

ART DECO TRUST
NAPIER, NEW ZEALAND
www.artdeconapier.com

Seventh Edition 2014

ISBN 0-9582030-9-1

Companion volumes to this publication are -
THE HAWKE'S BAY EARTHQUAKE
THE NEW NAPIER

AN ART DECO CITY

A small town in one of the remotest countries in the world, far from the European and American cities where 20th century design evolved, isn't the place where one would expect to find an Art Deco city. The style is generally associated with Paris, Manhattan, Hollywood or Miami Beach. Yet even in the early 1930s, New Zealand was only as far away from the civilised world as the time it took to mail an architectural magazine or freight a movie.

The Art Deco style had in fact made its appearance in Napier before its business area was wiped out by the massive earthquake and subsequent fires of 3 February 1931. On the whole however, in spite of a small building boom in Napier in the late 1920s, Stripped Classical and Spanish Mission were the favoured styles until the Earthquake wiped most of Napier's past off the slate and left its people ready to create a new look for the newest city on the globe.

WHY ART DECO?

Why was Art Deco so popular in the new Napier? There were three reasons.

Firstly, it was fashionable. The style had spread rapidly following the staging of the *Exposition des Arts Decoratifs et Industriels Modernes* in Paris in 1925, embraced by a world eager to adopt a new look to match the sweeping changes that were evident in social behaviour, technology and women's rights. Its adoption had been accelerated by the movies, which exposed it to small communities in remote countries within weeks of being seen in New York, Los Angeles or London.

Secondly it suited the need in Napier for a safe form of construction to protect the town from future earthquakes. The new buildings had to be of reinforced concrete, free of the decorative attachments that had fallen off and killed and injured so many people in the Earthquake. The low relief geometric patterns that were so much a part of the style were easily applied to the smooth concrete walls.

And lastly, it was cheap. Basically a concrete box, the typical building in Napier was a product of the Depression, which was at its worst in 1932 and 1933 when Napier was rising from the ruins of 1931. Worse still, many of the building owners in Napier had received nothing from their insurance companies, which deemed the quake to be an act of God, not covered by their policies. So owners had to borrow money to rebuild, while still repaying the mortgage on their non-existent pre-quake building. But a concrete box could be cheaply decorated to become a fashion statement, and in those times, before the Modern Movement had decreed that ornament was immoral, it was unthinkable to erect a building which wasn't decorated.

Safety and economy could also be achieved with the Spanish Mission and the Stripped Classical styles, both also in favour at the time, and so Napier, while having a predominance of Art Deco styled buildings, is in fact a catalogue of all of the styles fashionable in the 1930s, even managing to acquire, before the Second World War and the austerity which followed it put a stop to building construction for ten years, a few examples of the International Style. And it is unusual too in having buildings representing the Prairie style and the Chicago School from the mid-west United States. Together, they help to give Napier an architectural richness that is unexpected in a small town – a richness that inspired visiting Seattle based architectural historian Lawrence Kreisman to remark that Napier is 'a tapestry in which all the threads of the modern movement are woven together'.

THE 1931 EARTHQUAKE

The Hawke's Bay Earthquake was New Zealand's greatest natural disaster, in which 261 people are believed to have died, 157 of them in Napier, 101 in Hastings and 3 in Wairoa. Measuring 7.8 on the Richter scale, it was a massive earthquake by world standards. Its epicentre was 15 - 20 kilometres north of Napier, and its focus was shallow, at approximately 16 kilometres.

The first shock came with no warning, at 10.47am on a summer Tuesday, February third. After a pause of 30 seconds there was a second shock, ending $2^1/_2$ terrifying minutes after the first had begun. It was the first day of the school year and fortunately many pupils were outside, awaiting the commencement of organised classes. The town was busy, and it was there that most of the deaths and injuries occurred. If the shock had struck at night, the business areas of both Napier and Hastings would have been largely deserted.

Fires soon broke out, beginning for the most part in chemists' shops. In Hastings, where the water supply remained largely intact, these were contained. But in Napier, the water supply was broken and the fires destroyed what the earthquake had not.

The entire Napier area was tilted upwards by up to 2.1 metres, causing the water in the Inner Harbour, 3000 hectares of shallow tidal lagoon, to drain out to sea, creating a huge area of land which has been developed into residential and industrial suburbs, farmland, and the Hawke's Bay Airport.

THE RECONSTRUCTION

Most of Napier's residents left for up to two years while the town was rebuilt. Fortunately, planning was far-sighted and a moratorium on new building was imposed while decisions were made. A temporary shopping and business centre was built in Clive and Memorial Squares while streets were widened, street corners splayed, power and telephone lines buried (a rare thing then) and some design restrictions introduced, although these were modest, relating mostly to the height and design of verandahs which were required to be suspended from above.

Contrary to popular belief, there was no height restriction imposed. The low height of the new buildings was the result of psychological and economic pressure, after a major earthquake, during a depression. Some of the larger buildings were designed to have a third storey added as the need arose, although this has only been done in the case of Hawke's Bay County Council Building, now the County Hotel.

The new buildings were all constructed of reinforced concrete, the material which had proved itself in the earthquake. Decorated with low relief ornament, the city was uniquely colourful because with the exception of a few buildings designed by Louis Hay, which were faced in brick veneer, they were all of the same finish – cement plaster tinted with oxides in a wide range of colours which included cream, buff, ochre, pink, green and blue. Although there was a mixture of styles, the townscape was remarkably cohesive in scale, height and materials.

In January 1933, the almost completed reconstruction was celebrated by the New Napier Carnival. Further buildings were erected as the 1930s progressed, the last of them being in versions of the International Style, swiftly gaining favour overseas.

DOMESTIC DECO

The suburb of Marewa, which would have been reclaimed artificially, like Napier South, if the Earthquake had not occurred, was developed from 1934 on land which had been tidal swamp before 1931 and was deemed to be the property of the Napier Harbour Board. Many of its houses were in what we now call the Art Deco style, although they were known then as Spanish Bungalows.

Although such houses can be seen throughout New Zealand, they seem to have been more popular in Napier. It has been suggested that the rebuilding of Napier, and of Hastings too, in modern styles, propelled New Zealand towards a readier acceptance of modernism than was seen in most other countries. This seems likely to be true, and would logically have happened most in the town where it started. The result is a wealth of houses which in most countries would be considered radically modern, yet here they were not designed by avant garde architects for intellectual clients, but by builders for young working couples.

Certainly, in Napier they are more visible than elsewhere. This is partly because the availability of a large area of land not in private ownership, which meant that residential development in Napier was planned and built on a larger scale than in other towns of the same size. This, and the configuration of its coastal boundary, meant that almost all housing in Napier which was built between 1934 and 1980 is concentrated in large contiguous suburbs, each identified with a particular decade and cohesive in style. And the suburb which was developed in the late 1930s and 1940s was Marewa.

There are examples in New Zealand's larger centres of grand Art Deco houses, but in most cities, and in the small country towns where they can also be found, they are modest in scale – small three bedroom homes, built to a modest budget, for young couples starting out in life. Surprisingly, many of them have not been enlarged. Perhaps that is because during the 1960s, 70s and 80s when they had fallen from favour because of their uncompromising appearance, the owners felt inclined to move on to something more up to date. Yet some of those in Marewa were until recently still lived in by their original owners.

Many of the houses in Marewa are set in gardens which still bear traces of their original design, and are sometimes little changed. Severe, simple and relying on hard-edge trees and shrubs, either natural or clipped into rounded shapes, they reveal the way in which landscape design of the 1930s and 1940s was in harmony with the stark and uncompromising look of the domestic architecture of the time.

NAPIER'S ART DECO FRONT GARDEN

Napier is fortunate indeed to have a waterfront adjacent to the business centre that is not obscured by docks and warehouses, as is so often the case. Although not favoured with a coral strand or a beach of white sand, the blue South Pacific makes a spectacular backdrop to the formal gardens and their architectural features.

The Marine Parade was a narrow track on the edge of the beach until the 1890s, when the Sea Wall was constructed, using prison labour, to prevent heavy seas from breaking over the roadway and running down the main streets of the town. The Norfolk Island pines were planted at the same time, a perfect choice as it would turn out, to complement the geometric Art Deco style of the buildings to be erected 40 years later. Apart from the Municipal Baths (including hot water spa) of 1909, the paddling pool, the Swan Memorial Sunbay (1917) and a children's play area, the Parade would remain undeveloped for decades, although Mayor George Swan had envisioned as early as 1883 that Napier's sea front could become "a noble promenade".

Further development of the gardens began just before the Earthquake, when lawns were laid as part of a depression employment scheme. After the earthquake, the beach was used as a place to dump some of the rubble from the demolished buildings. From the Bluff Hill slip, which had been caused by the earthquake, clay was brought to create a level surface, then top-soil put on top of that. The gardens and lawns were completed by early 1933, by which time the city was largely rebuilt.

But as the 1930s progressed, the gardens continued to be enhanced mainly through the efforts of the Napier Thirty Thousand Club, formed in 1912 with the object of boosting Napier's population to that figure. The Kirk sundial, donated by the mayor of Gisborne, was built in 1933, and the following year, the Sunbay (now known as the Veronica Sunbay because the bell from HMS Veronica was for a time hung there) was built and the old Skating Rink, originally described as a concrete auditorium for dancing and skating, was laid. The Soundshell was built in 1935, and it was joined by the Colonnade and Memorial Arches, built in two stages in 1936 and 1938.

The two small arches commemorate the work of two stalwarts of the Thirty Thousand Club, Robert C Wright and Harold Latham, while the largest arch, the New Napier Arch, marks the creation of 'the New Napier', a term that was frequently used in the 1930s to distinguish the old city from the new. Etruscan in style, the arches are inscribed with noble sentiments which reflect the pride felt in the new city and the contribution and

sacrifices made by those who built it –"The pathway to power is through service", "Without vision the people perish", and "Courage is the thing. All goes if courage goes".

One feature not built by the Thirty Thousand Club was the Tom Parker Fountain, which was donated by Napier's premier menswear retailer, who had seen a similar one in Bournemouth in England. December 1936 was an exciting time on the Marine Parade as workmen raced against the clock to have both the fountain and the clock chimes on the T & G Building operative by Christmas. Both were completed in time, the fountain officially commissioned on December 23. From that time on, with the exception of the war years when blackouts were required, and then the immediate post-war years of power shortages when it played only on special occasions, its spectacular displays at night have been an enjoyable experience for residents and tourists alike.

1936 was also the year in which the coloured lights in the Norfolk pines were first installed, and these, with the electric lighting on the fountain, the soundshell and the other architectural features, made the Marine Parade a wonderland by night to Depression weary visitors to Napier in the late 1930s.

Today, these gardens and their architectural features constitute the finest waterfront in New Zealand, and one of world class. Contemporary with the reconstruction architecture, they provide a stunning theatre for the staging of civic events and an Art Deco front garden to the Art Deco City.

REDISCOVERY

Napier's pride in its modern appearance faded over the next two decades as war and the challenges of peace intervened and familiarity bred, if not contempt, then at least complacency. In the 1950s, 60s and 70s, an unconscious embarrassment about the low-rise townscape had crept in, reflected by the enthusiasm with which Napier greeted the construction of the two 'high-rise' (ie five storey) buildings that were erected in the 1960s. In the 1950s, Dr George Waterworth wrote in his memoirs that as he looked out over Napier from the hospital, he would often remark that "in Europe, they'd be fighting wars over this". But it was the view and the climate that he was referring to, rather than to the architecture, which had become passé, awaiting the cycle of taste to turn full circle.

That time was coming when in 1981, a group of OECD planners and architects passed through Napier and were impressed by its heritage buildings – not the three significant wooden Victorian examples that had survived the earthquake and fires, but "all the concrete buildings of the 1930s". Barry Marshall, who was at the time District Architect with the

Ministry of Works & Development, was struck by this and at the suggestion of Guy Natusch persuaded the Ministry to fund the publication of a book. The result was "The Art Deco Architecture of Napier" by Heather Ives. Following its publication, the Hawke's Bay Museum mounted an exhibition of the photographs taken for the book by James White, and soon after, New Zealand film-maker Peter Wells made "Newest City On the Globe", a documentary film for Television New Zealand.

A small group of people who were beginning to realise that Napier had something too important to lose – and potentially too lucrative to ignore – offered to stage a premier of the film in the Hawke's Bay Museum's Century Theatre, prior to its television screening. It would be preceded by a public walk through the city which would include jazz bands, vintage cars and street theatre. One hundred people were expected and two hundred catered for, but on a fine winter Sunday afternoon in 1985, eleven hundred people turned out, a demonstration of interest and support which would be deemed successful for any cause.

The rest is history. The Art Deco Group, as they called themselves, published a walk guide leaflet that year, began to conduct guided walking tours, incorporated in 1987 as the Art Deco Trust, and in 1992 began to operate full-time in high profile premises with professional staff. As the city's unique identity caught the imagination of the public, buildings were repainted in appropriate colours and civic pride swelled. Today the Trust is a Napier institution, of which a former

Napier resident has said, "It's no longer possible to imagine Napier without the Art Deco Trust".

But is this world-class heritage attraction safe? Sadly, no. In spite of City Council policies to encourage preservation, strengthened in the 2003 revision of the Napier District Plan, local government is unable to provide really adequate protection because New Zealand's heritage legislation fails to provide for it a firm legal basis for the preservation of built heritage, often dismissed as too young to be important. But it is only New Zealanders who dismiss it, not overseas visitors who recognise it as being comparable with other new world countries, and with old world countries too. Since 1983, when the National Bank and the Norwich Union Building were demolished, more than a dozen buildings have been lost or inappropriately altered within the Art Deco Quarter though none, fortunately, since 1985..

At present, Art Deco Napier's chief protection is public opinion, managed in the past by the Art Deco Trust but now to some extent self-generating as more and more people recognise that Art Deco has created civic pride, attracted hundreds of thousands of visitors, and put Napier not just on the map, but on the globe. The Trust's work in attracting tourists and publicity, providing interpretive programmes, mounting the occasional preservation campaign, working with the Napier City Council on guidelines, incentives and encouragement, and with building and business owners to increase their awareness of what the tourist wants and how to provide it, are just as important today as they were when the Trust was formed in 1985.

Daily Telegraph photograph

The demolition of the National Bank and Norwich Union buildings, 1983.

Napier's Art Deco architecture is enhanced by its beautiful setting, on the shore of the South Pacific. From the hill, sea views lie to the north, east and south-east, and the Mediterranean climate produces seas and skies of a stunning blue.

Napier's Art Deco style has become deeply embedded in the city's self-image and its cultural life today, best seen during the annual Art Deco Weekend held on the third weekend of every February.

THE MASONIC HOTEL

The Masonic Hotel (architects Prouse & Wilson, 1932) was probably Napier's most modern looking building when it was completed in 1932. Its first floor loggia is built out over the street, an unusual feature in New Zealand. This photograph was taken to publicise the 1996 Art Deco Weekend.

Clive Ralph photograph

The Masonic Hotel's sculptural parapet decorations, reminiscent of the thrusting radiator ornaments on cars of the Art Deco era, are unique in Napier. Embellishments like these were deliberately avoided after the earthquake, when many deaths and injuries were caused by falling ornamental features. But these ones are integral with the building's structure.

Below it, the entrance canopy with its glasswork incorporating Art Deco lettering is eye-catching.

The Daily Telegraph (architect E A Williams, 1932) is perhaps the most ebulliently Art Deco of Napier's buildings. Well endowed with the style's motifs – sunbursts, zigzags, ziggurats and fountain-like lotus flowers – it has had neon lighting added in recent years. This earlier colour scheme was based on the original colours of the building.

The two-storey high main office of the building was divided in half by a floor in the 1970s, but was restored in 2003. The glass block ceiling and the fine plasterwork on the beams and column capitals ceiling are now visible once again from the ground floor, and exact reproductions of the original pendant light fittings have been installed.

THE FORMER HOTEL CENTRAL

The Hotel Central (architect E A Williams, 1932) is a more delicate interpretation of the Art Deco style than the Daily Telegraph, although the architect was the same. A major feature is its balconies and balconets, with their angular arches and intricate zigzags and sunbursts.

On the stair landing is a lead-light window which echoes the shape of the building's arches and windows.

This design is one of a pair flanking the main entrance doors.

The capitals of the balcony columns are Egyptian inspired, with lotus capitals bearing winged falcon symbols.

The sunburst shape of the fireplace in what was the Hotel Central's lounge echoes the pattern of the glazing bars on the internal doors.

No photograph could illustrate better that Napier's historic buildings are not just a relic of the past but the hub of its commercial and cultural centre, still working for their living. This view of the Municipal Theatre (architect J T Watson, 1938) was taken at interval during an evening performance, before the 1997 addition of a larger foyer made the overflow of the audience into the street unnecessary. Above the heads of the crowd can be seen the Egyptian style columns and door lintels.

Because the theatre was completed six years later than most of the reconstruction buildings, it is different in a number of ways. Chrome hardware was used instead of bronze, there are hints of streamlining, and the lighting is more sophisticated with tubular and neon fixtures such as this dramatic ceiling light in what is now called the Port of Napier Foyer. The carpet in the theatre is an exact reproduction of the original cubist design.

Clive Ralph Photograph

"Aesthetically, it can only be described as regrettable", said Leo Bestall, Director of the Hawke's Bay Museum, describing the theatre in the 1950s. He was proposing that the City Council radically alter it, to improve its acoustics, sightlines and interior decor. By the 1950s, twenty years after its opening, its Art Deco style had fallen from favour and was considered to be in poor taste. No doubt the leaping nude wall panels, designed by the architect, were at the forefront of his mind. But like the movie palaces of the Art Deco era, the theatre had been designed to enable the theatre-goer to enter a fantasy world where everyday cares could be left behind.

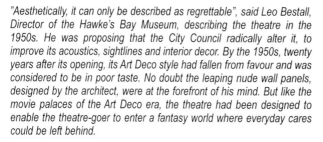

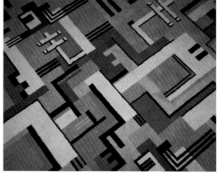

The exterior of the theatre after its major refurbishment programme was completed in 1997. During the 5 year project a new foyer was built, the backstage area was enlarged, the fly tower raised, performers' amenities improved, the proscenium widened, the stage area increased and the auditorium modified to suit modern fire and egress requirements and to improve the acoustics. The theatre was ready to meet the challenges of the 21st century.

OTHER ART DECO BUILDINGS

The Smith & Chambers Building (architect Alfred Hill, 1932), with its oddly shaped windows, has an appealing mix of decorative work with bold zigzags and a Mayan inspired flower and fern design.

Not far along Emerson Street at the Dalton Street corner, is Kidsons Building (architect Alfred Hill, 1932). The same architect has used a variation on the same zigzag motif, and again used interestingly shaped windows with angled glazing bars. The building's unusual plan is the result of the post-earthquake road widening of Dalton Street, where surviving buildings made it necessary to stagger the street boundaries.

The Hawke's Bay Chambers (architect E A Williams, 1932) is a typical example of the Napier variation of Art Deco – symmetrical, with ornament concentrated in the central bay which is the highest part of the facade. Its chevron glazing pattern is effective, and the interlocked letters HBC are reminiscent of the Ford V8 symbol which made its first appearance the same year as this building was erected.

The pressed metal underside of the veranda of the former Hotel Central has a pattern of stylised flowers and leaves.

ZIGZAGS –

At right - Hursts Building (architects Finch & Westerholm, 1930) was erected just before the earthquake, possibly Art Deco's first appearance in Hawke's Bay. Its sunbursts and zigzags typify the late 1920s Zigzag Moderne style of Art Deco.

At right & Below - Two variations of the zigzag, on the Chisholm Building (architect E A Williams, 1931) and the Sang Building (architect H J Doherty, 1932)

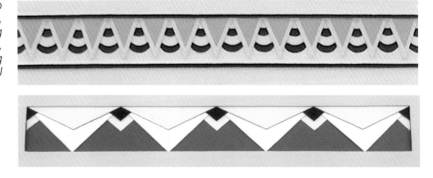

This pair of shop-fronts, in Ringlands Building (architects Finch & Westerholm, 1932), has joinery of 'Monel Metal', a patent alloy of copper and nickel, used before chrome plating was introduced. Both the floor and wall divisions are clad in terrazzo, a popular material still in occasional use, which consists of marble chips set into coloured cement on concrete slabs, and then polished smooth. This photograph was taken when a previous business occupied the premises.

Leadlight glass was a favourite form of building embellishment in the 1930s. This internal light was photographed when it was in the Callinicos Milkbar, (architect unknown, 1932), in Hastings Street. The Greek origins of its owners were acknowledged in the Greek motif on the façade. The building was demolished but its façade has been preserved in the new Farmers department store, and this window has been incorporated into one of the store's shopfronts.

One of the finest shop-fronts in Napier is in Harston's Building (architect E A Williams, 1932). The joinery is of oak, the entrances are deeply recessed, and the glass work has a hint of Charles Rennie Mackintosh. This photograph was taken in the early 1980s, when it was still Harston's Music Shop, owned by Neville Harston and his father since the 1920s.

The leadlight glasswork in the shop fronts of the Market Reserve Building (architects Natusch & Sons, 1931), is in the 'crown of thorns' pattern. This building, the first to rise in Napier after the earthquake, was designed the year before.

This mural in Market Street was designed and painted by Chris Finlayson in 1992. It portrays three visual art styles of the 1930s – painterly, graphic and poster art. Its title, "The City Beautiful", was the name of a booklet published in 1933 to mark the completion of the reconstruction.

Inside the Criterion Hotel building is this stunning window which stylishly summarises the Marine Parade – sea, sky and Norfolk Island pines. It was designed by Les Norwell, a draughtsman who worked for architect E A Williams.

Louis Hay designed the Earthquake Memorial at the communal grave at Park Island Cemetery in 1932.

The Deco City Pharmacy (architect Paris Magdalinos, 1985) is the most successful of the new buildings in Napier which have adopted aspects of the Art Deco style. It replaced a Spanish Mission building designed by Finch & Westerholm in 1932.

Hildebrandt's Building (architect Louis Hay, 1933) is unlike any of his other buildings. The flag panels on the façade were originally black and white banners, but the present owners have painted them in colours which represent the waves of the ocean uniting the flags of Wilhelm Hildebrandt's countries of birth and of adoption.

The seats and bollards in Emerson Street have been decorated by local artists. This design, incorporating the poster for the New Napier Carnival in 1933, was designed by Liz Earth. The inspection plate cover was designed by former City Architect Huub Maas.

The Taradale Town Hall (architect E A Williams), like the former Taradale Hotel, was built in 1932 to replace their two predecessors which had been totally destroyed by the 1931 Earthquake.

CLASSICAL REVIVAL & STRIPPED CLASSICAL

The County Hotel is the oldest reinforced concrete survivor of pre-earthquake days – at least part of it is. The corner nearest the camera was built in 1908 as offices for the Hawke's Bay County Council, and in 1935 it was doubled in size, keeping to the same style. It became a boutique hotel in 1994.

The Public Trust Office (architects Hyland & Phillips, 1922) pre-dates the earthquake by 9 years. Massively constructed, it survived more as a result of its bulk than its earthquake resistant design. It escaped the ravages of the fires and its internal oak fittings are still intact, removed and replaced after the building was strengthened in the 1980s.

The palm leaf capitals on the pilasters of Broadcasting House (originally the Dalgety Building, architects E A Williams, 1926) are evidence of the interest in Egyptian design after the discovery of Tutenkhamen's tomb in 1922. Its curved corner fore-shadowed the splaying of the street corners that was to take place after the earthquake.

Two Stripped Classical buildings appear in this photo. On the left is the office of lawyers Sainsbury Logan & Williams, which had its terra cotta coping tiles replaced in 2007. On the right is the former Kaiapoi Woollen Mills Building, now Forsyth Barr House.

The Spencer Block at the Napier Girls' High School (architect J T Mair, Government Architect) faces Clyde Road, on the Napier Hill. It was built in brick in 1930 and was damaged in the earthquake. In 1931 it was demolished and rebuilt in timber to the same design.

The Norwich Union Building (1932), originally the Bank of Australasia, was a charming Greek temple with Art Deco zigzags, iron work and interior plasterwork. Next door to it was the National Bank of NZ Ltd (1932), in Sripped Classical style with Art Deco friezes. Both buildings were designed by Atkins & Mitchell of Wellington and both were demolished in 1983. The two wrought iron grilles are now a feature in Herschell Street.

Photographs by James White

The former Bank of New South Wales (architects Crichton McKay & Haughton, Wellington 1932), has fern and flower decoration which is easily mistaken for Maori, sometimes considered to be in the Mayan style, but is possibly derived from French Equatorial African motifs seen at the 1926 and 1937 Paris Expositions. In the 1920s, American architects ornamented buildings with indigenous American art forms, usually Mayan or Aztec, instead of looking to European precedents. New Zealand and Australian architects, missing the point, often used American pattern books instead of utilising their own indigenous art.

ASB BANK

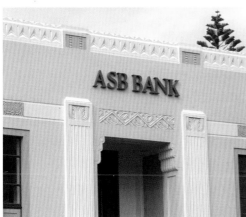

The ASB Bank, formerly the Bank of New Zealand (architects Crichton McKay & Haughton of Wellington), is probably the best example in New Zealand of a Stripped Classical building which incorporates Maori motifs. The exterior ornament is based on authentic whakairo (carving) patterns, and inside, the impressive coffered ceiling is bordered by kowhaiwhai (rafter) designs. Column capitals, grilles and other components of the building carry the Maori theme to a striking conclusion.

The parapet frieze on the bank looks typically Art Deco, but is actually an archaic Maori design.

A detail of the ceiling and columns.

The simple but striking Napier Antique Centre (architect E A Williams, 1932) was originally the Ross & Glendinning Building. It is one of four in Napier which is ornamented with Maori motifs, in this case kowhaiwhai patterns between the windows.

In 1936, the Temperance & General (T & G) Insurance Company erected this landmark building at the intersection of Emerson Street and the Marine Parade, providing Napier with a town clock. The building, which now contains restaurants, and accommodation suites, grandly closes the vista looking southwards alo ng the Parade from the northern end. The architects were Atkin & Mitchell of Wellington. In 2005 an additional floor was added.

The former Government Buildings (at the corner of Shakespeare Road and Browning Street) in what Americans describe as Graeco Deco style, was designed in 1936 by the Government Architect, J T Mair, but not built until 1938. In very Stripped Classical style, it incorporates an Art Deco entrance. Its exterior was the only post-earthquake building in Napier to be sheathed in stone, but wind erosion had caused so much deterioration that in the late 1980s it was repaired with cement plaster and painted. The severe, geometrically landscaped forecourt with its futuristic light house, was an integral part of the architect's design.

THE SPANISH MISSION STYLE

The palm trees of Memorial Square, which were planted when the square was laid out in 1920 in preparation for the visit of the Prince of Wales, make a perfect foil for the baroque Spanish details of the Provincial Hotel (architects Finch & Westerholm, 1932). This 1990 photograph shows the hotel in a previous colour scheme.

The Provincial Hotel features barley twist columns and wrought iron grilles over the entrance doors and fanlight, cleverly hinged to facilitate cleaning.

The balcony of the former Gaiety de Luxe Cinema in Dickens Street (architects Finch & Westerholm, 1931) shows its strong Moorish flavour. The cinema was built in the 1920s, but was remodelled when it was reinstated after the earthquake.

Until the 1920s, Toad Hall (originally the Empire Hotel, architects Finch & Westerholm, 1932) was a wooden building. When its rear section was destroyed by a fire, it was rebuilt in the Spanish Mission style. The front portion collapsed in the earthquake, enabling the reconstruction to be completed in the same style.

The State Cinema is now used for retailing, but this photograph shows it before the change. A rather Los Angeles flavoured example of the Spanish Mission style, it combined Spanish with Art Deco. Its interior, until its remodelling in the 1950s, was Napier's most Hollywood-like cinema, with coloured lights in fountain shaped wall sconces and female silhouettes flanking the screen.

A detail on Harstons Building. This facade was designed in Spanish Mission style before the earthquake, but was so badly damaged that it was reconstructed in the same style but to a different design. The structural framework of the building was 'caged', a technique that involved wrapping more steel around the beams and columns and pouring more concrete over them, to strengthen the structure.

The Criterion Hotel (architect E A Williams, 1932) is Napier's largest Spanish Mission style building, although with its Art Deco verandah profile and shop fronts, it is something of a hybrid. The tiled parapets and smooth walls are echoes of the original mud-brick 'adobe' walls of the Californian missions, protected from the elements by the tiles.

The Hog's Breath Café. (formerly the Napier Club, architect E A Williams, 1932) is the only free-standing Spanish Mission building in central Napier. This gives it an appearance more like the original mission stations of California which were the origin of the style. It even has a vestigial bell tower, in this case disguising a chimney; mission bells were used to call the native Americans to prayer or to meals when they worked on the mission estate. The brick arch with its sunburst outline is an appealing feature.

Bruce Jenkins photo

THE PRAIRIE STYLE & THE CHICAGO SCHOOL

This building, designed like all of those in this section by Louis Hay, was built in 1916 as a Soldiers' Club, but was better known in Napier as the Spa Private Hotel, named for its proximity to the hot salt water baths which used to operate as part of the Municipal Baths complex across the road, replaced in 2003 by the Ocean Spa pools complex. It is very reminiscent of some of Frank Lloyd Wright's houses in the mid-west in the early years of the 20th century. It has had many uses since the mid-1980s.

The passage way in the former Spa Hotel bears the stamp of Wright's work, in which parallel bands on column capitals were often seen.

The 1931 Pumping Station, at the Morris Street gates of McLean Park, was built as part of an upgrading programme of the water supply following its failure in the earthquake. It was restored and repainted in its original colour scheme in 1999. The handsome battered (sloping) brick wall beside it, also designed by Louis Hay, was built in 1937.

The Community Centre in Memorial Square, originally the Mothers' Rest, also has the look of Prairie style houses. Although altered several times, it looks remarkably unchanged since it was built in 1925.

The former Fire Station was built in 1921. The brick construction of the front section was damaged in the earthquake and it was demolished and rebuilt in concrete to an almost identical design. In 1969 a new fire station was built away from the city centre and the old one was converted into offices. The ornate details are similar to those on the original brick building and owe much to Frank Lloyd Wright.

Parkers Chambers (1929, reconstructed 1931) fronts two streets, and this is its rear facade in Herschell Street. Like Frank Lloyd Wright, Louis Hay favoured brick and used it as a veneer over the concrete structure of several of his buildings, often, as in this case, creating intricate patterns and using different textures to give a pleasing effect.

This is a detail of Hay's own building (1932) in Herschell Street, where he practised. Here he also used brick, mostly narrow Roman bricks, intricately detailed. The central emblem, similar to one on Desco Centre in Tennyson Street, is based on the original carpet pattern in the Robie House in Chicago.

Thorp's Building (1932), once the home of Napier's largest shoe shop, has a Mayan flavour. Its 'eyebrow', the ledge above the window, is seen on many of Hay's inner city buildings and is taken from Wright's Unity Temple of 1904-07 in Oak Park, a suburb of Chicago.

On the Abbotts Building in Hastings Street (1932), the grid-like patterns remind one of the work of Charles Rennie Mackintosh in Glasgow.

This detail on the Art Deco Centre echoes a 1930s radio set with its skyscraper ziggurat.

The Art Deco Centre, at the corner of Tennyson and Herschell Streets, was originally the Kinross White Building, built in 1932. Its interior was restored in 2012 when it became the home of the Art Deco Trust.

The Ellison & Duncan facade at Ahuriri was moved in 1994 when a town house development threatened it. Built in 1932 as the office for a wine and spirit merchant, it has been decorated with witty murals by Brenda Morrell. As on Thorps Building, the decoration has a Mayan flavour. In 2005 the facade was restored and the original colours, established from paint fragments, were reinstated.

Clive Ralph Photograph

Tennyson Chambers in Tennyson Street (1932), here seen in an Art Deco Weekend poster photograph, has a decorative device that is similar to the ornament on Wright's Unity Temple and also his Hollyhock House.

The long brick-veneered facade of Bowmans Building (1932) in Market Street shows off the 'eyebrow' and the geometric ornament tucked underneath it.

THE AMP BUILDING

The AMP Building, completed in 1935 for the AMP Insurance Company, is one of Hay's most impressive works. A blend of influences from Wright and Louis Sullivan, Wright's mentor, it also has some of the features seen on most of Hay's inner city buildings – the 'eyebrow' above the deeply recessed windows, a strong vertical emphasis, and decoration concentrated beneath the eyebrow. In this case, the decoration, which is more lavishly spread over the building, is similar to the Art Nouveau ornament which Sullivan used on his commercial buildings in Chicago. Perhaps this less modernistic decorative scheme was required by the client to reinforce their image as a long-established, prestigious insurance company.

The quality of the stucco ornament is superb, even on parts of the building some distance from the viewer.

The pendant lamps in the foyer are copies of the originals which were removed in the 1960s, although some are still in existence. Louis Hay designed them for this building, inspired by similar lamps in Wright's Robie and May houses of 1906 and 1908, and his Larkin Building in Buffalo of 1903-05.

Similar arched entrances to the two on this building can be seen on a number of Wright's early Oak Park houses. The oak storm doors are finely detailed, and the inner doors have etched and bevelled glass.

A view of the main entrance doors from within. The hardware on these doors was identified by the owner of a local antique shop, who had salvaged it when the doors were removed in 1973 and who donated it back to the owners of the building. The doors themselves had become the windows of a garden shed, and were recovered, refurbished and re-installed. The staircase (at right) had been altered in 1973, when the building was remodelled, but in 1992 it was restored to its original form. The balustrade is Art Nouveau and the plaster decoration is similar to some of Louis Sullivan's work.

MTG HAWKE'S BAY

The earliest section of the Hawke's Bay Museum and Art Gallery, built in stages in 1936 and 1937, incorporates another of the rounded arches favoured by both Wright and Hay. The entrance was converted into a truck dock in 1976 and the doors moved to a new entrance created when the Century Theatre was built. In 2013, as part of a major redevelopment of the institution, now renamed MTG Hawke's Bay, the original entrance was restored.

The lamps which flank the entrance are reminiscent of details in Wright's Midway gardens in Chicago of 1914, and were the inspiration for the lamp standards in Emerson Street, installed in 1991. By angling the reveals under the small windows and bevelling the corners of this building, Hay created an optical illusion which suggests that the walls are 'battered' (sloping back) in the manner of Egyptian temples.

In the Bestall Gallery, the magnificent internal doors with their intricately layered detailing, are a good example of Art Deco design and have been replicated in a new doorway on the opposite side of the room.

THE NATIONAL TOBACCO COMPANY BUILDING

Clive Ralph photograph

This superb building was known from the 1950s as Rothmans Building. It incorporates another rounded arch, this time on a grander scale and more Sullivanesque, inspired by arches used on a number of buildings by Louis Sullivan who liked the 'arch in a square' form which Hay has replicated here. The administration building, erected in 1933 for Gerhard Husheer, Managing Director of the Company, is Hay's tour de force, described by Carolle van Grondelle in the New York Times as a 'Fabergé jewel set in the industrial tundra of a seaside port'.

The wooden outer doors, carved by Walter Marquand, incorporate sunbursts and fruit within an Art Deco frame, and are flanked by stucco panels featuring native raupo (bulrushes) and roses, a favourite flower of Gerhard Husheer. The arch has a sunburst of Art Nouveau tendrils tipped by tudor roses, and the horizontal banding has insets of bottle green glazed tiles. The exterior colours have been loosely matched to the original tinted stucco finish, which although colourful in the 1930s, would be considered sombre for todays taste.

Roses can also be seen on the spandrel panels beneath the windows and in the superb bronze lamps, and grapes, similar to those on the AMP Building, are used in small panels high on the front wall.

The sumptuous interior has roses decorating the plaster ceiling and the bronze door hardware, and are combined with fruit in the leadlight glass windows, screen and dome. The wainscot is of imported marble. For a small town to have a factory office of such splendour is a rarity.

OUT OF TOWN

At Taradale, once a separate township from Napier, the Taradale Hotel (architect E A Williams, 1931) has started a new life as an Art Deco McDonald's Restaurant. This earlier colour scheme, prepared by the Art Deco Trust, was chosen to complement the McDonald's corporate colours. The cast iron rainwater heads bear the date 1931.

The Streamline Moderne style of Ranui Flats on the Marine Parade, designed and built by W J Green in 1938, has something of the look of the apartment buildings and hotels of Miami Beach.

In 1940, the hostel at the Napier Girls' High School was built, designed by the Government Architect. Although restrained in style, it boasts a superb Art Deco circular external stair, which is only visible from distant points on the hill.

Vetro, formerly the Richardsons Building (architects Natusch & Sons, 1932) at Ahuriri is a small but appealing touch of Art Deco in this industrial and maritime area.

Art Deco's last gasp in Napier, before the Art Deco revival began, was the Berry Memorial gates at the Napier Boys' High School, in Te Awa Avenue. Designed by J T Watson, they were built as late as 1958.

HASTINGS

Hastings is only 20 kilometres from Napier, and there too a rich architectural heritage was created out of the ruins of the 1931 Earthquake. Although the damage was not as severe as in Napier nor the fires as widespread, most buildings had their facades damaged or destroyed and the replacements created a stunning new townscape in the Art Deco, Stripped Classical and Spanish Mission styles, similar to Napier's townscape yet with its own character. Although there are fewer Spanish Mission style buildings in Hastings than in Napier, theirs are among the finest examples of the genre in New Zealand.

Las Palmas (formerly the Medical & Dental Chambers) in King Street North (architects Davies & Phillips, 1935) is one of the most appealing Art Deco buildings in Hawke's Bay and was sympathetically refurbished and re-landscaped in 2002. The low banded and curved garden walls give a hint of the Streamline style just appearing in New Zealand at that time.

Carlsson House in Warren Street North (architect Albert Garnett, 1933) is one of the most accomplished Art Deco style buildings in the city. Originally Carlsson Flats, it was converted into offices and renamed in 1987.

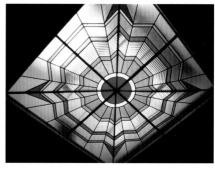

This laylight is one of two in Kershaw's Building in Heretaunga Street (architect Edmund Anscombe, 1932), and is similar to one in Harveys Building, now the Hastings Community Art Centre.

This former Bank of New South Wales in Market Street (architects Crichton McKay & Haughton, Wellington, 1934) was one of four bank premises designed by this firm after the Earthquake – the Napier and Hastings branches of the Bank of New South Wales and of the Bank of New Zealand. All except the Hastings BNZ are still standing. The verandah was added and the windows lowered in 1988.

The Dominion Restaurant in Heretaunga Street East (architect Edmund Anscombe, 1935) has the only shop front remaining of several in Heretaunga Street which featured an asymmetrical layout fashionable in the mid 1930s – a curved window on one side and a square set-back on the other. The interior has hardly changed in the more than 60 years since it was built.

The designs below typify the geometric patterns used on the many Art Deco buildings in Hastings, where decoration tends to have been applied with more vigour than in Napier. They celebrate the early 20th Century's love affair with jazz, the machine, technology, speed and progress.

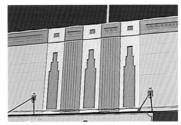

The former Hawke's Bay Electric Power Board building in Heretaunga Street East (architects Davies & Phillips, 1937) is sheathed in buff coloured terracotta tiles which have been overpainted. Terracotta, popular in the United States during the first half of the 20th century, was little used in New Zealand. The pilasters take the form of layered fins, a popular late Art Deco motif.

This quirky little building in Nelson Street South (architects Davies & Phillips, 1936), was originally Tong & Peryer's Funeral Parlour. Its asymmetrical facade is reminiscent of Los Angeles Deco.

The former Hastings Municipal Building at the corner of Heretaunga and Hastings Streets (architect Albert Garnett, 1917) is eclectic in style, perhaps reminiscent of India's Moghul style, and conveys the confidence of the expanding town of Hastings. The spectacular floral displays that are a feature of Hastings during the summer are evident in this photograph.

A number of stone bridges with an Art Deco flavour were erected in Windsor and Cornwall Parks during the 1930s, under Depression make-work schemes. The bridges, as well as walls and seats in other parts of town, were constructed of broken concrete slabs salvaged after the earthquake.

Hastings' Art Deco clock tower (architect Sydney Chaplin, 1934) was erected to house the bells from the old 1909 Post Office Tower which had collapsed during the Earthquake, throwing the bells across the intersection of Queen and Russell Streets.

This striking Art Deco residence in Pepper Street (architect Albert Garnett, 1935), was closely modelled on one built in Gisborne for Robert Kerridge, the cinema magnate. Its green stucco finish, a popular colour in the 1930s, is still original and its garden and front wall are all of a piece with the house.

The Hastings Methodist Church (architects Davis & Phillips, 1932) is the only church constructed in Hawke's Bay after the 1931 Earthquake in a contemporary style. Its interpretation of the Spanish Mission style is a simple one, contrasting with the ornate Mission details of the Theatre across the road.

The facade of the Municipal Theatre (architect Henry Eli White, 1915) is a richly ornamented, baroque interpretation of the Spanish Mission style. White's design was innovative, dispensing with internal columns except for a single, slender steel post supporting the balcony. The interior is in complete contrast to the exterior, ornately decorated in Art Nouveau plasterwork. In 2005 it was refurbished and decorated with stunning Klimt-inspired murals.

Peter Hallet photo.

Albert Garnett's 1922 building for Westermans Department Store was replaced by this magnificent structure (architect Edmund Anscombe, 1932), the jewel in Hastings' architectural crown. It is Spanish Mission from its Renaissance phase, rich with classical detailing. Under the verandah, with its pressed metal ceiling, is one of the most superb examples of shop-front design in New Zealand, in bronze, terrazzo and bevelled leadlight glass. Westermans' importance in the townscape is strengthened by its Spanish Mission style neighbours in Russell Street, possibly the most cohesive group of 1930s buildings in New Zealand. In 2001 the Hastings Visitor Information Centre moved into the building.

DOMESTIC DECO

Tom Parker Avenue was named for the donor of the fountain on the Marine Parade, who also donated the flowering eucalyptus trees in this street. This late 1930s house, still with its original garden design, is an excellent example of the Art Deco houses, known when they were new as Spanish Bungalows, which were popular throughout New Zealand.

This example, in Higgins Street, has the look of the bridge of an ocean liner. Nautical design was often an influence in the late 1930s.

In Morse Street is this uncommon weatherboard sheathed example. With no roof overhangs to protect the walls, wooden Art Deco houses required more maintenance than those of stucco or the more unusual ones of brick. But regardless of the exterior finish, the structure was of timber framing.

This very streamlined model in Kennedy Road also has a nautical air. Unfortunately it is now partially obscured by a fence.

This Higgins Street house is a hybrid of Art Deco and English Cottage styles.

This late 1940s house in Sanders Avenue, with a curved bay, has now lost its front garden. The front wall matches the house, a common feature. Town planning regulations of the period stipulated that front walls and fences should be no more than three feet high, to create an open, 'garden suburb' character.

This rare two storeyed example in Logan Avenue was built in 1950. Most of the houses built during the austerity of the 1930s and 40s were small in size.

These houses in Georges Drive form a handsome group, although they are not so eye-catching since two of them were painted in darker colours. Many visitors from Europe and America claim that they have never before seen so many Art Deco houses together.

THE MARINE PARADE

This classic picture postcard view looking south from the War Memorial was taken in the early 1990s, before the floral clock was relocated and the Soundshell repainted. On the third weekend of every February, this is the setting for the Gatsby Picnic, the climax of the annual Art Deco Weekend.

Photograph by Bruce Jenkins

Tourists enjoy meeting Napier's Art Deco man-about-town, Bertie, captured here by full moon with a friend.

The New Napier Arch and the A&B Building, from across the plaza which was once used as a skating rink. The coloured concrete finish on the paving has been largely worn off by the steel wheels of the skates used in the 1930s and 40s, although the view below of the Veronica Sunbay shows the Art Deco patterns in the paving.

The Veronica Sunbay, where the bell from HMS Veronica is hung for special occasions, was built in 1934. By the 1980s the sea air had caused its reinforcing steel, placed too near the surface of the concrete, to corrode severely. It was demolished and replaced by a new replica structure, for which the funds were raised by the Rotary Club of Napier. All of the Marine Parade features on this page were designed by Borough Architect J T Watson.

The Soundshell, built in 1935, was once the scene of regular outdoor entertainments, in the days when fewer people had cars and were more confined to the city in weekends and evenings. But it is still the place where citizens congregate when matters of civic concern arise, and the plaza facing it, with its surrounding architectural features, provides a superb theatre for ceremonial occasions, especially during Art Deco Weekend.

This hand-coloured postcard of 1936, photographed just after the completion of the Tom Parker Fountain, shows that apart from the growth of shrubs and trees and the removal of power poles, the area is little changed today.

At night the fountain is a spectacular focal point of the Marine Parade illuminations.

Both by day and by night, this historic park still conveys the pride and excitement that Napier people felt in the new city which they had created from the rubble of the old.

THE RECONSTRUCTION ARCHITECTS

There were four architectural practices in Napier at the time of the Earthquake, and almost all of the reconstruction work was undertaken by them, working together as the Napier Associated Architects. Sharing premises and facilities and working round the clock, they brought a unity of purpose to the immense task of rebuilding the town. But except in rare instances where a building might be designed jointly, each architect designed in his own way, each tending to favour a particular style.

The local practices were those of Natusch & Sons, Finch & Westerholm, E A Williams and J A Louis Hay. J T Watson arrived in Napier in 1933. Buildings owned by national companies, such as the banks and some hotels, were designed by the architects retained by those firms, in particular Crichton McKay & Haughton, Atkin & Mitchell, Prouse & Wilson, Stanley Fearn, Llewellyn & William (all of Wellington), L G West Son & Hornibrook of Palmerston North and Gummer Ford Hoadley & Budge of Auckland. The Government Building and the Telephone Exchange were designed by J T Mair, the Government Architect of the time.

Other buildings were designed by D B Frame, W Atherfold, Alfred Hill, H J Doherty, H Faulknor, A B Davis & Sons and R Holt & Sons. The Wellington architect Edmond Anscombe, who operated an office in Hastings in the early 1930s, designed two buildings at Ahuriri.

NATUSCH & SONS

Founded in 1886 by Charles Tilleard Natusch, who designed many large country houses in Hawke's Bay and the Manawatu area, this practice is the only one active in the 1930s which still operates today, as Judd Dougan Team Architects. CT's three sons Aleck, Stanley and Rene joined the firm which then had branches in Gisborne, Palmerston North and Wellington. Stanley, who practised in London during the early 1920s, brought back with him three folios of photographs of pavilions at the 1925 Paris Exposition of Modern Decorative and Industrial Arts and was no doubt influenced by those.

Buildings produced by this firm are typically restrained in ornamentation, and include the Market Reserve Building, Lockyer's Building, Blythes Department Store (now Nos 65 to 71 Emerson Street) and McGruers Building. The firm did much of the surveying and reporting of damage after the earthquake, and Rene Natusch was chairman of the Associated Architects. Stanley Natusch, who had a town planning as well as an architectural background, created the concept plan for the Marine Parade.

J A LOUIS HAY (1881-1948)

James Augustus Louis Hay, who was as a young man an articled pupil of C T Natusch, gave free rein to his admiration for Frank Lloyd Wright and Louis Sullivan. The work by Sullivan which inspired him dates from the 1880s and 1890s, Wright's Wasmuth Folio, a copy of which Hay possessed, was published in 1912 and depicted designs from the first decade of the century which are reflected in much of Hay's work.

Not surprisingly, his colleagues tended to consider his work rather dated at the time, but Hay's Napier buildings were of necessity simpler than those in the USA which had influenced them, and so must have seemed modern to his clients and to the public in the 1930s. Today, with their rich ornament, their association with Wright, who is now a cult figure, and because of the rarity of their type, they appeal to tourists in Napier as much as the most flamboyant of the Art Deco facades - perhaps even more so.

Hay's best known work is the National Tobacco Company building at Ahuriri. Gerhard Husheer, the company's founder, retained Hay to design all of the many buildings or alterations which he commissioned. Hay was chairman of the Hawke's Bay branch of the New Zealand Institute of Architects, and represented them on the Napier Reconstruction Committee after the earthquake.

One of Hay's articled pupils, Basil Ward, later joined fellow New Zealander Amyas Connell to form the now revered English practice of Connell Ward and Lucas, which designed some famous International Style houses there in the 1930s.

H A WESTERHOLM (1890-1972)

In 1932 Walter P Finch, a conservative architect who had been practising in Napier for a long period and had designed the Hawke's Bay Club in 1905, entered into partnership with H A Westerholm. Born in Palmerston North of Swedish and Finnish parents. Westerholm was considered progressive and was almost certainly the reason for the adoption of the Spanish Mission style which was used on a large number of the many buildings which this productive firm designed – they produced more buildings than any other firm during the reconstruction. The most notable examples were the State Cinema, the Gaiety de Luxe Cinema, the offices of Sainsbury Logan & Williams, the Shakespeare Hotel and the Provincial Hotel. Westerholm was also a versatile architect who designed freezing works and wool stores, as well as commercial and domestic buildings, and he also used the Stripped Classical style, examples being Forsyth Barr House and Bennetts Building. He moved to Australia in 1934.

J T WATSON (?-1960)

John Thomas Watson was born in Hull, England and came to New Zealand in via South Africa in 1905. He arrived in Napier in 1932 or possibly earlier. He designed almost all of the architectural features on the Marine Parade, as well as a few inner city buildings. He favoured the Art Deco style and in 1937 he designed the Napier Municipal Theatre after Louis Hay's original prize-winning design was rejected as too expensive. After some years in private practice he was appointed Borough Architect.

E A WILLIAMS (1875-1962)

Born in London, Ernest Arthur Williams emigrated in 1907. He set up practice in Napier in 1912 and being registered as both architect and engineer, he had many skills to offer after the earthquake. His reconstruction buildings include some of the most flamboyant Art Deco designs, such as the Daily Telegraph, Masson House and the Hotel Central and also some Spanish Mission designs including the Criterion Hotel and Harston's building. Stepped building profiles, intricate plaster decoration, the zigzag motif, and the use of Spanish balconies are characteristic of his work.

In 1939, his son Lawrence joined him in the practice and introduced the International Style to Napier with the Automobile Association Building in Herschell Street (now a backpackers Lodge). Ernest Williams' daughter Sheila, who was Queen of the New Napier Carnival held in January 1933 celebrate the reconstruction of the city, is commemorated in a bronze sculpture in Emerson Street.

NAPIER'S ARCHITECTURAL STYLES

ART DECO

The term Art Deco, coined in the 1960s, is today used to describe the many variations of the style which began to evolve around 1905 but became widely known only after the 1925 Exposition des Arts Moderne Decoratifs et Industriels in Paris. Encompassing the progression of the style from its early Classical influences, evident at the Exposition, through its zigzag, Egyptian influenced stage in the late twenties into the Streamline Modernes that held sway in the thirties, the term sometimes stirs purists to argue in favour of replacing it with the name Art Moderne. But it now has world-wide currency and any attempt to change it seems doomed to fail.

Broadly speaking, the style expresses the confident, brash and sometimes vulgar spirit of its age, when the excitement of speed and burgeoning technology, the social freedom of "the new woman", the relaxation of old standards promoted in particular by the movies, democratisation and personal freedom set the modern age well and truly on its path through the 20th century.

STRIPPED CLASSICAL

During the inter-war period, and particularly in the 1920s, classicism as promoted by the École des Beaux Arts in Paris maintained its popularity but in a stripped down version which suited the move away from Edwardian bombast. Classical details were reduced in number and became more bland, and deep set classical facades with a row of columns beneath a pediment were replaced by engaged columns or shallow pilasters. In Napier, a comparison between the Public Trust Building of 1922, Forsyth Barr House of 1932 and the former Government Buildings, of 1936, shows the progression from deep to low relief ornament and less of it.

Stripped Classical may also incorporate indigenous, modern or even Art Deco ornament, to a point where it might be termed by some to be an Art Deco building. The ASB Bank, the Crombie Lockwood Building and the former Government Building in Napier are examples of this.

THE INTERNATIONAL STYLE

At the Bauhaus Design School, founded in Germany in 1919, the philosophy of "the building as a machine" was adopted and stark structures of steel, glass and white concrete began to come off the drawing boards. By 1930, the style was making an impact in Britain and Europe, and from the mid-thirties in the United States, where some of the Bauhaus leaders took up residence after the Nazis closed the school. Bauhaus designers considered that ornamentation was not only unnecessary, but inherently bad. Form should follow function and an object designed to do its job well must automatically be beautiful. The name "International Style" was given because the style was used world-wide without consideration of local techniques, materials, climate or culture.

The earliest examples of this style seen in Napier are the former AA Building in Herschell Street (1939), the 1954 wing of MTG Hawke's Bay on the corner of Herschell and Browning Streets (modified in 2013), and the former Nurses' Home on the corner of Chaucer Road North and Napier Terrace on Hospital Hill (1952). All of these were designed by Lawrence Williams, and none are illustrated in this book.

SPANISH MISSION

Originating in the south-west states of North America, the Spanish Mission style was popular in new world countries, especially those with climates similar to California. It arrived in New Zealand in 1913 when the Auckland Grammar School was completed, and in Hawke's Bay with Iona College in 1914 and the Hawke's Bay Opera House, Hastings in 1915.

By the 1920s, Spanish Mission had become extremely popular in Southern California, because it reflected the Spanish heritage of the American south-west and because it was promoted by cement manufacturers as suiting eathquake-proof reinforced concrete construction. It was used in many of the homes of movie stars and also for hotels, theatres and even for Los Angeles' Union Station. The style is characterised by smooth cream walls, which echo the lime-washed mud brick walls of the early mission stations, clay-tiled parapets to protect the walls from erosion by rain, small square or larger round-arched windows, balconies, and the usual elements of Spanish ornament – inlaid tiles, wrought iron, and sometimes baroque decoration.

In 1931, before Napier's reconstruction commenced, suggestions were made that the "Spanish style", as used in Santa Barbara following its earthquake of 1926, would be suitable for Napier and would bring a harmony of style to the city. The idea did not take root, but to most people, the buildings which we now describe as Art Deco were rather Spanish in style, and were often described as such, or as "Free or 'Modern' Spanish style" in contemporary newspaper accounts.

THE CHICAGO SCHOOL AND THE PRAIRIE STYLE

The classification of buildings in the Chicago School and the Prairie style often overlaps, since features of the first, which is most associated with Louis Sullivan's work in the 1880s and 1890s, were often seen in early examples of the second. In Napier, courtesy of Louis Hay, both styles are found. The Chicago School can be seen at its best in the National Tobacco Company Building, which uses Sullivan's favourite wide, round 'arch in a square' form. The AMP Building has Sullivanesque Art Nouveau ornament, tighter and more intricate than the loose free-flowing European Art Nouveau, combined with the smaller round arches which are typical of early Frank Lloyd Wright buildings, designed soon after he left Sullivan's office where he worked and studied.

Wright's Prairie houses are echoed in the Community Centre in Clive Square and the former Spa Hotel at the north end of the Marine Parade which was built in 1916 as a soldiers' club. And on many of Hay's non-residential buildings, the projecting flat roofs or the horizontal ledges giving protection to the deep-set windows, the geometric decoration, and the raised bands giving panelled effects to the rough-cast stucco walls are all typical of the Prairie style, which although usually associated with Wright, was practised by a number of mid-western architects early in the 20th century.

ACKNOWLEDGEMENTS

REFERENCE SOURCES

Peter Shaw & Peter Hallett:	"Art Deco Napier", pub. Art Deco Trust, 6th edition 2009.
	"Spanish Mission Hastings", pub. Art Deco Trust, 2nd edition 2006.
Heather Ives & James White:	"The Art Deco Architecture of Napier", pub. Ministry of Works and Development 1982
Daily Telegraph:	Issues of the 1930s
Art Deco Trust:	The Art Deco Inventory, compiled by Tom Gill & Amanda Bullman, pub 1991
Note:	Where the date of a building is given, it is the date of completion.

PHOTO CREDITS

Photographs by Peter Scott and Robert McGregor for the Art Deco Trust, except those otherwise acknowledged which were taken by Clive Ralph, Peter Hallett, Bruce Jenkins, the late James White, and by Warren Buckland for the Daily Telegraph.

Cover Photo – Jeff Brass